The Roaring Twenties

Marketing & Selling Better in the Post-Pandemic Decade

Shawna Suckow,
CSP, CVP, CMP

The Roaring Twenties: Marketing & Selling Better in the Post-Pandemic Decade

Copyright 2021 by Shawna Suckow International

All rights reserved. No part of this book may be reproduced or transmitted in any form or by any means without written permission from the author.

ISBN 9798507254842

Published in the United States of America by Porcus Volanti Press

For Jack

Table of Contents

Psst...have your device handy and open YouTube – this book has interactive case studies!

Introduction	7
Section 1: The Roaring Twenties!	11
Section 2: Changes are Afoot	31
Section 3: Tools & Strategies	75
Section 4: Predictions for the Future	143
From the Author	154

Introduction

 Get to know your 1920s phrases!

'The Bee's Knees' Something fantastic.

"Wow, fellas, see that dame? She's the bee's knees!"

In early 2020 I was looking forward to a year of the highest earnings I had ever booked as a professional speaker. I was excited to get back on the road after the holidays—being busy and rushing through airports and reaching platinum status on Delta again. I looked forward to being able to take a couple international trips to speaking engagements that were far flung (and definitely squeezing in a vacation or two to recuperate). Life was fast paced, and I loved it.

The pandemic changed my priorities so much as a mom, as a wife, as a speaker, and as an employer of others. For the first time in my life, I slowed down enough to enjoy gardening and putting together puzzles when, just six months prior, I made fun of my sister-in-law, because she had the patience to assemble a thousand pieces of a picture. For fun. And then, puzzles became a form of therapy for me. Maybe the world wasn't making progress, but I could at least see progress in something tangible. I know it might sound lame, but I also know I wasn't alone because puzzle sales went through the roof during the early days of COVID. Admit it, you became a bigger nerd, too.

Think about your journey from March 2020 until now. How many times have your priorities and your focus shifted? How are you a different person today? You're not alone. The entire world has shifted, and in this book, I'm going to do a deep dive into one particularly major shift: consumer behavior. Understanding this will result in easier, more successful sales and marketing for you and your company.

Two good things about the pandemic:
1) It's mostly behind us
2) It's set us up for a decade that's going to be as wild as the 1920s a hundred years ago.

I'll discuss new ways to use old sales and marketing strategies. I'll give you some fresh ideas to try. I'll leave you with some predictions for the future. And in between, I'll even teach you a few handy phrases from the first Roaring Twenties (you know, just in case they make a comeback).

Let's go!

SECTION ONE: THE ROARING TWENTIES!

Get to know your 1920s phrases!

'Iron one's shoelaces'
To use the restroom.

"Excuse me, fellas, I gotta go iron my shoelaces!"

*Bonus points if you can work any of these 1920s phrases into normal conversation in the next 48 hours.

Welcome to the Roaring Twenties (The Sequel)!

"It was way better than the first Roaring Twenties!" said hopefully all of us.

Think back to your high school history class and conjure up an image in your mind of women's suffragettes. Women in long white dresses with cinched waists, bustles, and giant hats over their giant hairdos.

That was just before the Roaring Twenties. Just *two years later,* women were wearing short hair and even shorter hemlines, and smoking (gasp) and drinking (double gasp) in polite society. What a huge cultural shift in a very short time.

No cultural symbol of the 1920s is more recognizable than the flapper. A young woman with a short "bob" hairstyle, cigarette dangling from her painted lips, dancing to a live jazz band. Flappers romped through the Roaring Twenties, enjoying the new freedoms ushered in by the end of the First World War and the dawn of a new era of prosperity, urbanism and consumerism. – www.history.com

In an interesting parallel to today, society was emerging from a pandemic in 1918-1919, but they also were emerging from the added trauma of the first world war. They were ready to go outdoors safely again, celebrate life, and reconnect with other humans. Sound familiar?

Picture a rural farmgirl moving from the Midwest to L.A. – that's the type of major cultural shift I'm talking about, but instead of one farmgirl, it was the entire nation going through such a huge shift in perspective and norms a hundred years ago. It was that sudden, and that transformative.

These are similar times, my friend. We are in for some serious excitement, a huge cultural renaissance, and fast-paced change.

Compounding the end of the wartime economy was the spread of the so-called "Spanish flu," a virulent contagion which not only killed hundreds of thousands of Americans from the fall of 1918 to the spring of 1919, but shuttered businesses from coast to coast.

Incredibly, the dire post-war economic predictions didn't come true. At least not immediately. American consumers, who had patriotically scrimped and saved during wartime, began to live it up. Europeans also joined in, purchasing $8 billion in exports from America. Inflation ticked upward, and so did prices, but consumers were willing to pay anything for a taste of freedom.

– James Grant, www.history.com

We may not have been through a world war, but we've been through a lot of social trauma: the isolation of the pandemic, political polarization, racial struggles, and infighting with friends and family about it all.

2019 was a dumpster fire for many. I remember when the new year began, many were posting on social media things like, "Well, I'm glad 2019 is over – 2020 is going to be SO much better!" Little did we know.

It's no surprise we're ready to break away from the angst of these past couple years with renewed hope and a return to financial stability for many, coupled with a desire for less worry, more freedom and more fun.

The 1920s experienced a cultural, artistic, financial, and social renaissance, and we're poised for the same. It's going to be a wild ride, and I can't wait!

A Brief History of Time (Well, at Least This Century...)

Don't skip this part like a high schooler just skimming before a test! It's important for context.

Have you ever been in the ocean when a giant wave comes up unexpectedly and does a full body slam on you? You knew there would be periodic waves, but this one was different. Maybe you even got tossed around a little (or a lot), and it took you a hot minute to gather your bearings?

Well, that's how I believe most of us have felt after each of the three major economic, societal, and personal waves (more like tsunamis) that have hit us this century. We were dazed, confused, and more than a little 'shook' as my teenager would say (did you feel that? Somewhere out there, my son just cringed and rolled his eyes).

The First Wave

The terrorist attack of September 11, 2001 terrified Americans to their core as the first foreign attack on US soil in modern history. Americans had never felt so vulnerable at home. It absolutely changed our culture in a permanent way and impacted the rest of the world to varying degrees as well.

For the purposes of this book, I want to focus on one part of that change: why we as consumers shifted how we behave and buy.

Americans were afraid to go to large venues or travel for quite a while after 9/11 because of uncertainty if those places would be targeted by an enemy that was still unknown to us.

As a resident of Minnesota, I live close to the Mall of America. We would often go there on the hottest summer days, and the coldest winter days, to get a respite from the weather. Thousands would crowd the mall to be able to walk around indoors and interact with other humans, but when 9/11 happened, we assumed the Mall of America was almost certainly a target, as an undeniable symbol of American consumerism.

I'm sure you remember where you were when the planes hit the Twin Towers, and how you felt for weeks or months afterward.

We all stayed home quite a bit for weeks after 9/11 as fear kept us from our everyday lives.

"For obvious reasons, commercial and crowded venues such as malls, movie theaters, trains, buses, restaurants, and hotels are prime terrorist targets. These are the very places we frequent as consumers and so, after an attack, we naturally experience a loss of control. After all, people just like us have suffered terribly, even lost their lives, for no other reason than being in the wrong place at the wrong time while doing normal, everyday things. Could this happen to us the next time we are in a store, on a train, or watching a movie?"

– www.PsychologyToday.com

The ripple effects on sales & marketing were enormous. We saw a major uptick in consumer use of the Internet, which was still in its early years. According to Pew Research, in the year following 9/11, about a tenth of Internet users started doing some things online that they would have done offline before the terror attacks occurred. For many, this meant shopping on the Internet *for the first time*. Can you imagine? Yes, I can, because I am old(ish).

Welcome to the dawn of serious e-commerce. This meant that immediately post-9/11, many brands increased their online presence (remember the clunky old websites of yore?), and companies of all kinds began to increase their use of email to reach prospects. 'Hooray,' we thought, 'a cool new way to connect with buyers! And they all open the emails!'

If you're 'vintage' enough to remember the movie 'You've Got Mail' from 1998, there was a time when getting an email was an electrifying experience. It happened so infrequently that we had a little computer voice that notified us every time our inbox got some action. Can you imagine today if you had a little voice annoying the crap out of you every time you got an email? But I digress…my point is that email was entering its heyday for salespeople, and 9/11 gave it a huge boost (like the boost Zoom had during the pandemic, but more on that later).

Immediately after 9/11, if a company didn't have an online shopping cart, they were at a disadvantage. Can you imagine today having to call a company to make a purchase? Egads.

While all this was happening, consumers started to seize the day and shop like it was their job.

"...in the aftermath of 9/11, American consumers heeded President Bush's call to go shopping "and enjoy life, the way we want it to be enjoyed" by buying homes, cars, appliances, furniture, and electronic gadgets in record numbers.

There are also a number of studies which show that exposure to thinking about death leads to heightened materialistic behaviors and lowered concern for others or the environment. In one survey conducted in 2003, consumers who were more fearful of becoming a terrorism victim were more interested in buying branded goods and were also likely to consume compulsively."

-www.PsychologyToday.com

Sound familiar? The pandemic months saw a huge uptick in spending for those who were able to do so. Home improvement stores had record years, and the luxury goods market was strong. But again, I'm getting ahead of myself.

To summarize: we discovered new ways to market and sell in the early 2000s, while consumers were eager to part with their money. It was a good time to be in business once we got our bearings again as humans after the attack.

The Second Wave: The Great Recession

Let's take a look back now at the second great body-slamming wave of the century: The Great Recession of 2009-2011. Ugh.

There were massive job losses. In many cases entire corporate departments were reduced to just one or two employees holding down the fort.

B2B salespeople became increasingly desperate to meet quotas, so they were doubling and tripling their outreach efforts. Budget cuts meant no tradeshows, no travel, and fewer resources for sales efforts.

The result was a massive increase in the cheapest, quickest form of prospecting: phone calls and emails. The sheer volume was unsupportable by the prospective customers (remember, they were fielding all emails and calls for their former colleagues as well as their own). In no way could these buyers keep up with the new demands of their increased workload, let alone the new flood of incoming sales messages.

Put yourself in the shoes of one buyer. Every salesperson she's ever known reached out to her, and hundreds more on top of that, overwhelming her. She couldn't possibly keep up, so she started to ignore the voice mails and emails. She no longer would politely reply. She simply didn't have the bandwidth.

I hear lots of older salespeople gripe about how buyers these days just don't have the common courtesy to respond, even with a quick "no thank you." I hope you can see why, now. It was salespeople who changed B2B buyers forever, due to the sheer flood of outreach during the Great Recession.

Once the recession ended, buyers had become used to not responding to the flood of cold outreach, and they never returned to their old ways.

The shifts that we saw take place during that time are still evident today in how easy it is for most of us to ignore phone calls and emails, especially those that seem impersonal or ill-researched to us.

Couple that with the fact that younger generations are just innately averse to talking on the phone or using email (anyone have teenagers?), and the modern result has been staggering.

We've saw a major shift in how the most effective B2B salespeople prospected from 2012-2019. Prospecting by telephone had become a dying art, although some people still swore by it. As I always say, if it's working for you, great – keep it up. But for the rest, it became an annoying requirement by sales management, and it no longer worked. It was a huge waste of time when other tools were becoming far more effective.

Similarly, massive, impersonal email blasts were losing effectiveness every day. Think about your own behavior over the past decade. In the morning, you'd wake up, grab your phone (that is probably charging on your nightstand) and open your email. You swipe away anything resembling a cold email or an email blast, save for the few that you actually recognize and want to read. Apps like Unroll.me now help millions of people unsubscribe to blasts every day.

Email blasts became a dying marketing and prospecting tool as well. Millions of sales professionals blamed themselves, wondering if they weren't working hard enough or weren't targeting the right people, or weren't using the right language. Wrong. It wasn't you (most of you, anyway), it was the tools that were becoming obsolete.

Enter the Third Wave.

The Third Wave: The Pandemic

Fast forward to 2020. Along comes the Third Wave to body slam us yet again and throw us into the proverbial oceanic churn of confusion.

This wave would amplify everything that shifted in the past two crises. What's a salesperson to do? How are marketers supposed to reach prospective audiences in the 'New Normal' (cringe)? That's what this book aims to tackle.

This seems like a good time to introduce you to the drinking game I invented during the pandemic. On every Zoom call, every webinar, every virtual conference at which I spoke, I asked the audience to take a drink every time someone said a cringe-worthy pandemic word or phrase. Popular examples: Pivot, Unprecedented, and New Normal. Depending on the time of day, I usually drank water, but hey, you do you.

There's already so much evidence in how companies need to shift to stay relevant.

These are definitely unprecedented times (drink) and the overuse of catchphrases like 'unprecedented times' became antiquated in a matter of weeks, not months or years. Everything was moving quickly as we all sought to pivot (drink).

All the things that marketers and salespeople said at the beginning of the pandemic soon became outdated or even annoying and turned buyers off. Even though their intentions were good, marketers had to shift more quickly than ever before, to keep up with the changing marketplace.

In fact, the pandemic accelerated changes quicker than any previous national or world event in my lifetime. Technology, fashion, shopping, finance, politics – the impact has been tremendous and quick, kind of like, well, a giant wave coming out of nowhere.

"In the world of commerce, the things we thought we would see in 2030 are now things that we're seeing today. At the beginning of this thing, we as a company decided to kind of blow up our roadmaps. We deleted all of our plans," said Arpan Podduturi, Director of Product, Retail at Shopify.

- www.Forbes.com

These massive waves of change have led us through 20 years of unimaginable upheaval and evolution: political, cultural, financial, and social. When our customers change and evolve, we must do the same.

The pandemic accelerated everything about customer behavior. Things I didn't expect to see for another decade are happening now.

I'm going to focus on how customers everywhere have changed, so anyone in sales or marketing can adapt their strategies to be more successful with less effort. Sound good? Great – let's move on.

SECTION TWO: CHANGES ARE AFOOT

Get to know your 1920s phrases!

'Icy mitt'
Getting rejected.

"Poor fella, he thought she was the bee's knees, but she gave him the icy mitt!"

That College Psychology Course is Finally Coming in Handy

Most of us experienced a psychological rollercoaster during the pandemic, and it has had some lasting effects on consumer behavior. I want to talk now about Maslow's Hierarchy of Needs. You might remember this from your high school or college years if you took a psychology class. Your professor would be so stoked!

"Maslow's Hierarchy of Needs is a motivational theory in psychology comprising a five-tier model of human needs, often depicted as hierarchical levels within a pyramid. From the bottom of the hierarchy upwards, the needs are: physiological (food and clothing), safety (job security), love and belonging needs (friendship), esteem, and self-actualization.Needs lower down in the hierarchy must be satisfied before individuals can attend to needs higher up."

— www.simplypsychology.org

Why is this important? Because it absolutely sets the stage for how consumers are making decisions and setting priorities. Never in modern consumer history has the entire emotional load of the world played such a factor into shifting our behaviors.

Maslow's Hierarchy of Needs

9/11 was certainly an intense period of change, but not as starkly evident as here in the United States. But the pandemic – oy. I can't remember anything comparable to the pandemic in my lifetime. It has so permeated every country, every generation, every population across the world, regardless of nationality, wealth, gender, etc.

Sure, the pandemic has impacted generations differently as it's ravaged the elderly segment most of all. The poor also have been more at risk, but truly, throughout the pandemic, everyone has had to assess their own mortality to some degree and the risks that they were willing to take to live their lives.

As a result, it makes perfect sense to turn to Maslow's Hierarchy of Needs to understand our prospects and the audiences we try to reach. If we don't understand their mindset and their motivators, how can we possibly rise above the noise and get them to pay attention to us?

Looking at the bottom level of Maslow's Hierarchy of Needs, you can see that everybody's basic initial concern as human beings is food and shelter. Nothing else matters if you don't have your very basic needs met. If you're experiencing homelessness or food insecurity, you're likely not thinking about your next vacation or paying college tuition.

If you are worried about securing your next roll of toilet paper or feeding your family, you can't be worried about buying your next set of appliances. A salesperson trying to push a product or service that isn't directly relevant to their prospect at that time (i.e. toilet paper vs. appliances), isn't rising above the noise.

Does that mean that someday this prospect could become viable again? Certainly, they can, so don't write them off if they can't buy from you this very moment – remember that cultivating the relationship is still important.

I saw a lot of tone-deaf marketing attempts at the beginning of the pandemic, where organizations either decided to keep running the same ads regardless of the historic change in the world emotionally and physically, or they just decided to pull an ostrich head-in-the-sand moment and go on pretending that life was normal or would return to normal soon.

Well, we all wished that life would return to normal quickly, but that wasn't what happened. What we felt emotionally was the very baseline of Maslow's Hierarchy of Needs. We saw a rush to buy basic supplies, like toilet paper, and stock up on food staples.

People around the world were concerned about very basic human physiological needs, and those of their immediate family. We circled the wagons, so to speak. I brought my daughter and my bonus son home from college, my teenager's school closed, and we stocked up on essentials.

Only when people were becoming more assured that toilet paper still existed and food was still available did they rise to the next level of the Hierarchy where they could focus on safety.

As soon as they no longer had to risk personal safety to make purchases, that's when we saw the retail sector start to bounce back as companies started to adapt to the headspace of their customers. The greatest success came to those who understood that their customers needed their basic needs met but didn't feel safe doing things traditionally.

Savvy retailers immediately pivoted (drink) to offer curbside pickup and home delivery, and to ramp up their regular online shopping options. Those who were slower to adapt paid the price.

 Case Study

There are two gas stations near my house, across the street from one another, and they both have similar offerings. They both have small convenience stores as well as gas and basic staples. There wasn't much of a reason to

have a preference of one versus the other unless prices were significantly different in gasoline or something of that nature. It was just a matter of habit for customers.

During the pandemic, one of those gas stations was very quick to adapt and the other was not. The one that was quick to adapt was thriving. Throughout the pandemic, it was always full of cars even though as a whole, we all were using less gasoline.

It was obvious that the gas station that adapted was making their customers feel safe enough to make a quick run for milk there, as opposed to maybe going to a grocery store or waiting for delivery. The other gas station didn't do so great of a job conveying their safety measures, and ended up closing for several months.

When the other gas station finally opened five months later, they had to put up a huge sign that said, "WE'RE BACK!" Interestingly, their lot is mostly empty to this day, while across the street, the competition's lot is mostly full. Habits changed in a short amount of time. People developed routines and decided that they appreciated the gas station that stayed open and made them feel safe and met their basic needs. Their loyalty was earned. It was that quick.

If you didn't keep in touch with your customers to support them and adapt to their needs during the pandemic, you had—and have—an uphill struggle. I completely understand. I found it very difficult to focus on prospecting and marketing during the pandemic. Hopefully our customers haven't switched to the competition and gotten comfortable.

This is not to say that restaurants, businesses, and other organizations did anything wrong if they couldn't survive, because some just could not get the numbers needed to make sense or to even pay their basic workforce. You may have been furloughed as so many were. I don't blame companies that had no choice in the matter. I am pointing out however, that this pandemic changed your customers forever.

In times of crisis, consumers change their behavior very quickly as we've seen. Companies and retailers that were able to adapt quickly survived, and some even thrived.

Case Study

My husband works at the corporate office of an upscale bed manufacturer. I'll call them Shleep Number. Even though millions were out of work during the pandemic, companies like his thrived. They shifted their marketing in time to capture the disposable income of those who weren't struggling. They shifted their store safety protocols quickly. They ultimately had their best financial year in the history of the company in 2020.

Many industries and companies experienced a similar ride. Home improvement, ecommerce, and grocery delivery services to name a few.

We've all seen companies that were too late to the game, though. I hope yours wasn't one of them. Of course, many industries had no choice to close-up shop. As a professional speaker, I went from having my best year ever, to my worst year ever—in a matter of two weeks. We all drive by stores and restaurants that couldn't make it, through no fault of their own.

Clearly, the impact of the pandemic will be long lasting. The shifts in buyer behavior have been vast and are not over. Therefore, the shifts that we need to take are not over.

We must continue to pay attention. What worked in the first month of the pandemic turned off buyers in the second month. Remember when words like 'pivot' and 'unprecedented' didn't make you cringe? About a month into the pandemic, those words became ridiculed, much to the dismay of marketers everywhere.

What worked in the second month was no longer appropriate six months later. The toilet paper jokes were no longer relevant, for example.

My point is that consumer behavior will continue to change, so don't get comfortable! It's a time to continuously adapt your messaging and your strategies, more often than you did in the past.

I realize that this makes it very difficult to be in sales and marketing. I have every sympathy for those who have been at their wit's end multiple times throughout this collective human experience we've all endured.

I commend those who have had the energy and strength to continue to adapt. It is after all, the only way to keep moving forward as we continue into the Roaring Twenties.

Splinter Groups

This pandemic experience, which I've taken to calling the 'Collective Human Meat-Grinder,' forced several interesting cultural shifts. One of those is the creation of splinter groups that have divided our culture. It's important to understand these because every prospect and client of yours fits into several of these, as do you.

Here's just a sampling of new divisions that arose between strangers, colleagues, families, and friends during the pandemic:

- Science vs. religion
- Science vs. politics
- Politics vs. religion
- Masks/social distancing vs. personal freedom
- School closures vs. working parents
- Mandated bar/restaurant/event closures vs. patrons, owners and employees
- Geo-political differences, i.e. the state or area you live in may have approached the pandemic very differently than others.
- Truth vs. conspiracy
- Introverts vs. extroverts (the impact of

working from home)
- Adult children vs. elderly parents
- 'Real' news vs. 'fake' news
- Opinion vs. fact
- Economy proponents vs. safety proponents

I've never experienced a time of so much divisiveness in my lifetime. Certainly, there have always been political differences, but the pandemic challenged everything from long-standing institutions to family ties.

This is important because these splinter groups have changed the way we need to market. A one-size-fits-all approach no longer works the way it used to. Even when talking about subject matter that used to be a given in society (i.e. the polio vaccine is good! Let's all get the polio vaccine!), you now can offend anti-Covid vaccine proponents. It's best to stick to the communication strategies I reference later in this book until you get a better idea of where your prospects stand.

More Changes Underway

Consumers initially shifted their buying behavior out of necessity due to store closures and new ordinances. Home delivery became the norm, and for some, it will be a permanent change. If you didn't have a compelling online presence before – one that truly helped you stand out from the competition—then now's definitely the time to catch up.

Working from home changed the face of the traditional office and will forever resonate with many companies. Why continue to rent expensive downtown offices when the pandemic has shown the boss (and he finally believes it) that the workforce can be just as productive from home?

Add political divisiveness and permanent cultural shifts to the mix, and the world is forever changed.

You may as well throw away your marketing and sales playbooks from 2019 and 2020. It's definitely a whole new era, and I'm not even sure adapting is enough. It's almost like we have to start from scratch and build a whole new model.

In my marketing sessions today, I talk about throwing away the box. It used to be the trendy thing to discuss thinking outside the box vs. inside the box. The term 'outside the box' should be banned because it's so overused, and now I believe it's outdated. In fact, add that phrase to the drinking game I discussed earlier.

It's clearly time to throw away the box. The box was destroyed during the pandemic and is no longer usable.

Pandemic Upstarts Gain Momentum

An interesting trend that I noticed after the Second Wave of the 21st century—the Great Recession—was that it really shifted a lot of people into working for themselves. It created a huge number of entrepreneurs and gig workers.

Plato said, 'Necessity is the mother of invention.' I think the necessity of losing your corporate job is the mother of a lot of new entrepreneurs.

The pandemic is forcing another evolution of that same movement. As people either were furloughed or laid off, the shift to becoming more self-sufficient through entrepreneurialism gained steam again. So many simply don't want to be at the mercy of another company ever again, if they can avoid it.

"America is currently experiencing what some are calling a 'startup boom.' That's right — even with a raging pandemic and an ugly recession, America is seeing a boom in the creation of new businesses.

John Haltiwanger, an economist at the University of Maryland, has been working with the U.S. Census Bureau to measure new business creation for decades. Every new business that hires workers, he says, has to apply for an employer identification number with the government, and when the coronavirus pandemic began, the data showed what you might expect: "We saw a collapse in new business applications," Haltiwanger says. But then, about six weeks into the pandemic, the numbers started rising. At first, he says, they had to double-check that the data were correct: "We were, like, what's going on here?"

And then the new business applications just kept rising. "The third quarter of 2020 is the highest quarter of applications we've ever seen," Haltiwanger says (their quarterly data go back to 2004).

Most of these new businesses are seizing opportunities created by the weird coronavirus economy — an economy where people don't really want to do stuff face-to-face anymore. The largest area for new business creation is online retail. Of course, at the same time, we've seen a massacre for brick-and-mortar retail — and we don't know yet whether these new businesses will fill the job void. Moreover, many of the new businesses are just people who were laid off and were forced to strike out on their own. But with these important asterisks, it may be good news that new businesses are growing out of the ashes of old businesses."

'The Unexpected Boom in Startups'
November 10, 2020
--www.npr.org

Why does this matter to you? Because it's more important than ever to stay in touch with your customers and prospects as they switch companies, positions, industries, or even start their own ventures. In many cases, they'll be able to do business with you again, introduce you to their replacement at the old company, or refer you to others based on the strength of your relationship.

 Case Study

As the founder of a professional association, I saw an interesting shift happen before my eyes

between 2010-2012. A full third of our membership worked for corporations prior to the Great Recession. Over those years, while the members stayed mostly the same, the pie chart changed pretty dramatically. The slice that was corporate members shrank, while those same members became entrepreneurs and decided to consult, contract, or compete on their own. The membership today remains largely the same, with those members still performing the same work in the same industry; however, the members themselves are now independent contractors or small business owners doing the same work under their own flag.

Sadly, many salespeople wrote off these new solopreneurs and upstarts simply because they assumed there was no potential there. What's important to note is that many of the corporations who laid off those people enlisted the very same people as contractors. The corporations were – smartly but perhaps unethically – getting the same people without having to pay for their employee benefits, and without having to train newcomers.

The bottom line is this: don't write off upstarts or individuals just because they're no longer on a corporation's official payroll. As solopreneurs, they may work for multiple corporations, and actually control more business now than before pandemic!

Here are just a few of the companies that were created during the Great Recession:

- Facebook
- Airbnb
- Warby Parker
- Credit Karma
- WhatsApp
- Venmo
- Instagram
- Uber
- Pinterest
- Slack

If you were a salesperson who brushed off these upstarts and their founders when they left corporate America, I bet you'd feel pretty dumb right about now. Believe me, I hear from my association members all the time that their memories are very long – especially when it comes to being abandoned by those they considered supplier partners before.

Also, keep in mind what a fellow speaker once said: "I'd rather have someone refer me five times than buy from me once." That has stuck in my head as a rule to live by in sales.

Keep in touch with your best customers, even if they change jobs or start their own shops. And don't write off a prospect just because you think they can't afford you or maybe they've said they can't afford you.

It never hurts to build that relationship anyway, because referrals will become more important than ever, as prospects continue to become better than ever at ignoring sales & marketing efforts.

Here's the buyer journey as it currently stands:

1) We buy from people we know and like.
2) When that's not possible, we ask people we know and like for recommendations.
3) When that's not possible, we trust complete strangers on the internet who say things about you or your company (reviews).
4) When that's not possible, we start from scratch and do our own research.

Sometimes it's a combination of all the above. Keep in touch with those existing relationships – it will be the differentiator more so now than ever before.

Work Itself Looks Different Now

Remember the days in sales where it was a pleasant surprise to your customers when you would do a 'pop-in' visit? You'd show up unexpectedly with brochures and maybe some donuts. Those days were over before the pandemic for most of us because it annoyed our prospects, but now those days are over for just about everyone. You can't do a pop-in when someone works from home – that would be weird.

The traditional office has changed forever during what has been deemed the Fourth Industrial Revolution, which was defined by www.weforum.org as "a moment in time when increased automation, artificial intelligence (AI) and continued technological disruption will fundamentally change the way we live, work and relate to one another."

Of course, nobody could have foreseen the rapid shift to working at home that erupted during the pandemic. Most white-collar workers pulled up a desk at their home office during lockdown, and have continued to work remotely, proving to grumpy old bosses everywhere that it could be done.

"The blurry lines that already existed between work and personal life have been all but obliterated during the pandemic. Without the time spent commuting in the morning and at night, people are logging on to work earlier in the day and staying connected later into the night.

Beside the cost savings of operating a scaled-down office or no office at all, modern technology and communications have allowed workers to stay connected, collaborate from afar and be more productive without lengthy commutes. Parents are also clamoring for more flexibility to care for their children.

"...people can be more valuable in how they work, which doesn't really matter where you spend your time," said Alexander Westerdahl, the vice president of human resources at Spotify, the Stockholm-based streaming music giant that has 6,500 employees worldwide.

"The change is mainly driven by globalization and digitalization, and our tools are much,

much better at allowing for people to work from anywhere," Mr. Westerdahl said.

- www.nytimes.com
'Remote Work Is Here to Stay.
Manhattan May Never Be the Same.'

This change has benefitted so many workers: parents, those with long commutes, and disabled people. I would venture to say that nothing has empowered the disabled community more when it comes to work opportunities. I have a disabled friend who was able to begin work as a customer service representative from her home—working for a company that had never allowed such a crazy practice! (pssst...guess what? It's working!)

Our Culture is Forever Changed

One of the few bright spots of the pandemic was that companies finally caught up to the desires of their customers and employees. I've already touched on the shift to allowing at-home work, which has benefitted so many individuals and families. Hopefully savvy businesses will realize the incredible benefits outweigh their desire to have their employees visible and in cubicles at all times (can you guess where I stand on this issue?).

Another bright spot was that retailers everywhere finally granted customers the option to buy from their sofas and have same-day delivery. Amazon started this craziness years ago when they introduced the then-unheard-of two-day delivery. It was sheer madness! Years later, they unrolled same-day delivery and consumers everywhere went berserk.

It was high time that other retailers caught up and began to offer a service that customers have clearly wanted for years.

'You mean I can have my kalamata olives, new spatula, and glue gun delivered today?!' Yes, Phil, yes you can.

Sometimes it takes a huge push to get companies moving in the right direction. Then, it takes savvy leadership to not pull it back and return to business-as-usual.

The Death of Professionalism

I've been speaking to audiences about the slow death of professionalism for several years now, but the timeline of its demise sped up tremendously in 2020.

The decade-long trend toward greater authenticity has long spelled doom for professionalism as we know it. What we used to tolerate as 'unprofessional' we now accept, and even welcome.

I've worked from home since 1999. I remember in the early years I would cringe whenever a client would overhear one of my kids or dogs on a phone call. I bet 99% of us were on a Zoom call during the pandemic where a kid or dog interrupted, and it became a topic of conversation – just two humans relating. It wasn't as embarrassing as it was pre-pandemic. We don't go to the same lengths to sequester ourselves away from our personal lives before hopping on a Zoom or phone call anymore.

I would now say that having such interruptions is humanizing for the salesperson and removes the Sales vs. Prospect invisible barrier. Suddenly, you're just two people laughing and trading stories about interruptions, or kids, or cats.

There's an interesting theory about sales, having to do with our lizard brains. Back in the early days of human beings, when we fought prey or became prey on a regular basis, we had instincts called Fight vs. Flight. You've heard of it, and we still have those instincts even though most of us no longer hunt saber-tooth tigers.

Well, in a sales conversation, the salesperson is the hunter, and the prospect is the prey. The prospect is on guard, keeping up the fight-or-flight instinct until something comes along to make them feel safe. What better way to ensure that than a dopey Golden Retriever jumping on mom's lap during a Zoom call, I ask you?

When my Golden Retriever, Henry Jones, Jr., interrupts a video call or phone call, I explain that he is my Director of Barketing (yes, he's even listed as such on my website, www.shawnasuckow.com). It usually results in a great laugh, and a great conversation where I immediately have become a relatable human, not just another speaker looking for a gig.

I believe the death of professionalism is a win for sales professionals who can leverage it to get past the initial Wall of Hesitation (I just coined that phrase – I think I'll keep using it).

Generally speaking, professionalism is slower to die out in older generations. They were raised differently, and have spent most of their careers behaving professionally, so it makes sense they would have a harder time letting go. Generation Z – the youngest generation currently in the workforce – would naturally have an easier time letting go of behaviors they've only recently adopted.

So, this of course, depends on who your prospects are. If your customers tend to be younger, you especially need to reflect their more casual leanings. If your prospects tend to be older, test the waters by being a little less formal.

What does the death of professionalism mean for those of us in sales and marketing? It means that we need to a) understand and b) reflect back the changing mood and tone of our prospects.

Those who are slow to adapt to this more casual way of being are going to have trouble rising above the noise. And believe me, there's a lot of noise out there right now, as desperate salespeople and marketers are doubling and tripling their efforts to try to reach prospects.

But you do not have to double or triple your efforts if you're working smarter. And that means really homing in on how your prospects are thinking and feeling, and reflecting that.

As a whole, thanks to the pandemic, our entire society has become more casual—one of the few positive impacts of 2020.

This means the way that you write, dress, and talk have to change or you're unrelatable and out-of-touch to your prospects. You don't want to come across as old-fashioned or stuffy in the Next Normal (drink).

Writing & Talking Differently

We've been trending toward more casual writing for many years now, but so much of this accelerated during the pandemic. Many people began working at home for the first time, and the ongoing jokes on social media focused on wearing sweatpants on Zoom calls. And not being able to remember the last time you wore nice shoes because you'd been wearing slippers or flip flops or going barefoot. And women complaining that all their makeup was expiring and going unused. It's been a collective human experience worldwide, and it's a relatable topic for all of us.

In fact, I made this fancy line graph for one of my speeches:

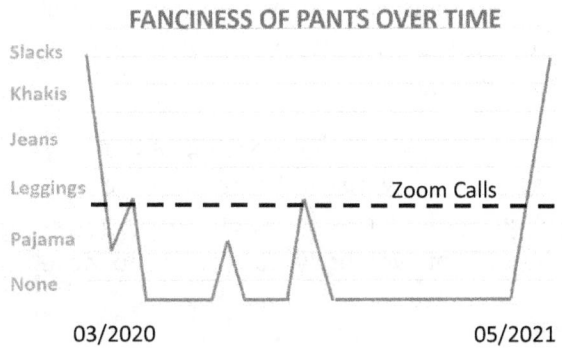

Picture this: your prospect is at home, with kids bouncing off the walls, just trying to get work done. They're fitting work in between laundry, online grocery shopping, and letting the dog out.

Now here you come along with a really formal, outdated email or marketing piece. They cannot possibly relate to you! You're just making it easier for them to ignore you.

Finding what's relatable – finding the common threads in this shared human experience – and leveraging those to make real connections is the way forward. This is not changing back to the old formalities after the pandemic.

Tuning into your prospects' daily reality means you're less likely to be tone-deaf in your outreach. Remember when 'pivot' and 'unprecedented' used to be great words that didn't evoke a cringe from every living human? Anyone still using those words is out-of-touch with how those words now fall on their prospects' ears.

Believe me, I was guilty of saying all those cringe-worthy words and phrases at the beginning of the pandemic. But I quickly realized that everybody was starting to make fun of them and so I needed to shift my language.

That's what I mean by reflecting how your prospects are thinking and feeling, so you're not out of touch. Thankfully, it's easier than ever now, because the pandemic gave all of us permission to speak and write less professionally.

During the pandemic, I wanted to convey empathy for our shared human struggle, but I had to figure out how to convey it differently in my marketing materials to a) not evoke the cringe, and b) rise above the collective noise to get noticed. I continued to just talk like a normal person and say things like, "Wow, this really sucks not being able to see our co-workers. Wouldn't it be nice if you could 'pivot' (yes I said it) and find better ways to connect?"

What I was selling was my unique way of engaging people through virtual platforms like Zoom, where people aren't just talked AT.

As a professional speaker, I had to adapt and develop new ways to deliver my content that didn't suck the life out of Zoom audiences like some speakers did/do. My marketing had to reflect that. I'd never get past the gatekeeper if my outreach was boring and non-engaging, so I had to walk the walk, and talk the talk.

That became my differentiator, because my competitors were still sending out boring, lifeless, overly-professional emails and phone calls that totally missed the mark. Their prospects had completely changed. The good news for me is that most of my competitors are still doing it!

My advice to you is to communicate in a natural way, like you're talking to a friend. That grabs people's attention in a very humanized way and stands out from all the salesy competition.

Think about how you would introduce your friend in a bar. You'd speak casually, friendly, maybe inject some humor. When you're communicating to a prospect, think about your product/service/company as your friend in a bar.

Good Bar Introduction: "Hey my friend, this is Jack. I've known him for a million years. We used to work on a farm together in Iowa every summer when we were kids."

Bad Bar Introduction: "Dear Mr. Jones, I'm pleased to introduce you to my friend, Mr. Jack LaFollette. We've spent many years developing our friendship, and I believe you'll find him to be worthy of your time."

See how the second one is completely tone-deaf for the situation? I get countless emails every day that sound like a bad bar introduction. The ones that stand out are simple, human, and a little fun.

Here's the best prospecting email I received during the pandemic:

Hey First name - haha, just kidding!

Hey Shawna! 😁

We don't know each other, and unwanted emails suck, so here's a cute picture of my dog, Rebb, wearing my slippers from a few days ago.

Hopefully that buys me 5 more seconds of your time to actually tell you why I'm emailing you ;) I'm founder & CEO of [EmailAnalytics](), a tool that lets you monitor your team's email activity, and shows you stats like emails received, emails sent, and average email response time.

Email response time is critical for sales teams. 35-50% of all sales go to the vendor who responds first. EmailAnalytics is how you measure and improve it.

We have a 14-day trial (no card required) if you want to check it out!

*And use code **REBB** to upgrade to PRO on the house.*

Cheers,

Jayson

I'm sure some (older) folks found his language way too casual, so of course this goes to 1) knowing your audience, and 2) being bold enough to stand out, knowing that you won't impress everyone, but you'll sure stand out to way more people than the competition. You can't build a large prospecting pool if you're afraid to stand out.

Dressing Differently

Like most of you, my dressier clothes...ok, anything with buttons or zippers, let's be honest...languished in the back of my closet for over a year. I lived in athletic gear, even on days when athletic activity wasn't even a passing thought. I made the messy bun a work of art (not a Van Gogh, more like a Dali or a Picasso).

During the pandemic, many of us developed a style I like to call the 'Pandemic Mullet': business on the top half, leisure on the bottom. Perfect for Zoom calls!

I do believe, though, that we're all wanting to feel more civilized in our attire as we emerge from the pandemic, but that it'll be short-lived. It seems antiquated now to return to dresses and suits – like a throwback to a bygone era. It'll be occasionally fun to dress up (hey! Shoes with heels!), but it won't be a complete return to the norm. I'm predicting we'll get a bit dressier for conferences and important meetings, but it won't be long-lived for us or our clients. That'll reinforce the trend toward all of us dressing more casually.

My suggestion, like always, is to reflect your clients and prospects. How do they dress?

A few years ago, I spoke to a group of bankers in a midwestern state. The bank manager came up to me afterward, aghast. He shared that he'd been requiring his staff to wear suits and ties all these years. He realized during my session how off-putting that must've been for the farmers coming to the bank. He changed his policy to allow his staff to dress more casually going forward, to totally change the tone of the bank and their relationships with customers. Bravo.

In summary, we've been headed down the road toward business casual for quite some time before the pandemic, and I see that trend continuing.

SECTION THREE: TOOLS AND STRATEGIES

Get to know your 1920s phrases!

'Sinker': A donut.

"I can't believe this dame's making so many sinker references in this book. She must be zozzled!"

Psst! You there! You're halfway through the book now. You'd be the bee's knees if you would write an Amazon review for me when you're done!

What Tools are Working?

"Finally, she's getting to the good stuff!" said every reader. I hear you. The first sections were important to give the context (and also give you ammunition to take to your boss if he/she isn't keeping up with the shifts underway. Handy tip – leave an anonymous copy of this book on their desk!).

What are some of the tools that you can use now for prospecting now that your buyers have changed so much?

You'll be disappointed to learn that there are no new magic bullets that have been invented, unless you want to start using drones to deliver donuts to prospects (hey, now there's an idea!).

But there are ways to rethink how to use the tools you already have available.

Cold Calls? Meh.

Some people still swear by the cold call. If you have success at picking up the phone and just dialing for dollars, by all means, keep on keepin' on. There was a time during the pandemic where we all were longing for human connection. I had a deep conversation with a Verizon guy one day when I called in for service, for example. Generally speaking, we seemed to pick up the phone a little more and be a little kinder to strangers trying to sell us things. We were not as busy, some of us were quite lonely, and it was a strange departure from cold-calling reality. But that time is over.

As we emerge from the pandemic and get back to "busy," we'll return to ingrained habits of ignoring sales calls and only returning voice mails that serve an immediate need.

Especially for those of us who continue to work at home, we have a different human mindset because of our surroundings, and different distractions. We may have children and pets in the background, we may be outside working at the park, or the local coffee shop, or at an Airbnb somewhere remote. We may be working irregular hours because we do our best work at midnight.

It's going to be harder than ever to reach people by phone going forward. My recommendation is to spend your time on things that get better results.

Emails? Only if done correctly.

Refer back a few pages to the email I received from Jayson. It got through my cluttered Inbox and grabbed my attention because he took the risk of being different. I can't stress this enough! Continue to email like an overly-professional old-timer at your own detriment. Continue to send out cringe-worthy, pitchy emails with salesy language if you want to be ignored.

Reach out and truly connect in a human way to rise above the noise and get noticed! Risky? Somewhat. Can you please everyone? No. Will you engage with far more people? Absolutely. Getting them to even open your email today is 90% of the battle.

Once they open it, the challenge becomes a different one: getting them to like and trust you, so they take the next step. One unique way I've done this with my staff is through their signature blocks.

Most email signature blocks are mundane, containing the same set of details as the next. Why not mix it up a little to stand out a lot?

 Case Study

Tracey is a retired friend of mine. She most recently was the executive director of a North American association of meeting planners called SPIN. As the Founder of this association, I wanted to let everyone know that we were different. I decided to have some fun with each staff member's signature block.

I wanted everybody on our staff to really showcase their personality, starting with not using a professionally posed photo. I asked them, "What imaginary Olympic event would you receive a gold medal in?" I also asked, "what's something random you excel in?" Here are the results:

Tracey B. Smith, CMM, CMP
Executive Director

Gold Medalist in Guacamole Making | I excel at: impatience and chasing shiny objects

www.spinplanners.com

Ask me about the best conference I've ever attended. Go on, I dare you!

There are ways that you can humanize yourself and your staff that are free, that really get

prospects to let down their guard. Tracey got more requests from strangers for her guacamole recipe than she was prepared for. Guacamole for the win!

Video email? Yes!

Video email burst onto the sales scene a few years ago. I've been touting it to my audiences, but I have very few who actually adopt it as a prospecting tool, which is absolutely crazy. Video email is hugely impactful, and will transform your business results, guaranteed. Why? Because it's so unique that prospects are still curious enough to open and view the messages.

Before the pandemic, Dubb (my preferred video email service) reported that video email was 67% more effective than regular email. 67 percent – that's crazy! But by all means, continue to send out all those traditional written emails (she said snarkily).

There are tons of video email services out there right now. You definitely want to use a service rather than recording a video on your phone and just attaching it to an email, because an attachment is going to end up in people's spam. Many of the professional providers have been white-listed so that they get through spam filters (yet it still appears as if it came directly from your email). They also send your video as a link, not an attachment, for space reasons.

The recipient doesn't see it as a scary-looking link; they see a preview of your video – a two-second clip of you, looping over and over again in their Inbox.

For that reason, whenever I start a video email, I wave and hold up a dry-erase sign with the recipient's name on it, so that that's the two-second clip they see when they open my message. They are far more likely to open that video and watch it, especially knowing it was personalized and made just for them.

There are free video email services out there, but make sure yours notifies you when your video is watched. This helps with timing of your follow-up communication. Once my video has been viewed, I follow up with a regular phone call, because at that point, they know who I am.

Case Study

A few years ago, my sales assistant, Rachel, decided to give video email a try. She's not a professional speaker and, like many, wasn't super comfortable starting a one-way conversation in front of a camera.

Here's a link to one of her earlier attempts at prospecting. Watch this, and pay attention to the huge shift that happens at the end:

 bit.ly/youtubeshawna7

The best thing about that video was the end when she broke from her professionalism. This is really a metaphor for everything I'm trying to convey in this book! We break through, connect better, and become more memorable when we simply give up the uber-professionalism and take the risk of showing our humanity.

Did Rachel send this video email? You bet she did, and she got a great response from the prospect. She since has gotten far more comfortable with video email, and she's more casual and conversational now. In fact, some of the time, she is even holding her baby when she's doing these videos, because she's allowed to be human. People have babies. People are working from home more and more now. It's okay.

The ongoing results: Rachel has been more successful working fewer hours because the time she spends prospecting is far more humanized, resulting in greater efficiency now.

Referrals

If you're not keeping track of referrals and incentivizing referrals, and really going after referrals, you're doing yourself no favors in the post-pandemic age.

The association I founded has a members-only Facebook group, where I'm able to keep a finger on the pulse of what these business buyers are thinking and feeling. Keep in mind that all business customers are regular consumers in their off hours, so there's not a huge gap in behavior between business-to-business and business-to-consumer when it comes to how the buyer thinks and feels – especially post-pandemic.

In this Facebook group, during the pandemic, the members went through an actual grieving process, which I believe we all did as humans. As members of the live meetings industry, things were dire in the group. I could tell the moment when hope was starting to return because they started asking for referrals again. Members started to post requests for recommendations more frequently. 'Who do you use for this service?' and 'Who do you buy this product from?' and 'What hotel do you recommend in Tampa for a meeting of 300 people?'

You can bet that that this same grieving process happened in most industries, most families, most groups of friends. When people are ready to buy again and they're being extra careful with their money, they're going to do even more research than before. And they're going to put a lot of stock in the opinions of people they know. Be one of those people. Be a person that a lot of people know and would recommend. Stay top of mind, and be sure your connections truly understand what you do and *what your ideal client looks like*.

Reach out to your favorite customers and ask for advice. Asking for advice triggers something in the recipient! Tell them what your ideal prospect looks like. Ask for introductions and recommendations. To make it super easy for them, ask for three contacts you can reach out to, and permission to use their name when you do. Believe me, if they're happy with you and what you've done for them, most of them will give you names if you simply ask. Others will prefer to make the introduction themselves. Either way = win!

Ask for video testimonials. Ask if you can tag them in a LinkedIn post, thanking them for being a customer. Ask for advice about where to find cool clients like them. Then reciprocate.

LinkedIn

I spoke with a friend toward the end of the pandemic, and she told me about her new focus on LinkedIn. She had never really paid it much attention, other than creating her profile page. During the pandemic, she decided to spend time seeing if LinkedIn was worth the effort.

I'll begin with the end: over half of her business now comes directly from LinkedIn, after just six months of gradual build-up.

Here's what she did:

1. First, she updated her dusty old profile. She humanized her Summary section with a story of how she got to where she's at now, and *why she loves what she does*. She used a little humor and ended with a sentence about how she likes to spend her time when she's not working. You don't have to get fancy or elaborate. This is an easy formula to follow.
2. She updated her Headline section, which is the only thing people see about you besides

your photo when you post something or reach out to connect. It tells exactly how she solves problems. It does NOT include her work title, i.e. 'VP of Sales.' This is prime real estate in your profile, so use it smartly! What problem do you solve, and for whom? Mine says 'Obsessed with helping orgs understand shifting consumer behavior caused by the pandemic. Certified Virtual Presenter, Global Speaker, Exceptional Parallel Parker.'

3. She started posted a question daily, and still does. Some questions are professional, some just for fun. When someone responds to a question, it boosts her visibility thanks to the LinkedIn algorithm, so even the personal questions are important (and guess what? They get the most engagement!). Sample professional question: What drives you to do what you do? Sample personal question: who are you looking forward to connecting with the most, once you're ready to travel again?

Tips:

- Use a service to schedule batches of posts in advance, so you don't have to physically

be on LinkedIn everyday unless you want to (when someone responds to one of your posts, it helps to respond back fairly quickly).
- Include at least five hashtags in each post, at the bottom. These can be the same hashtags every time, if you like. Choose hashtags based on the audience you want to discover your posts.
- In the beginning, if your posts aren't getting a lot of traction, create a LinkedIn pod. That's what I call a group of your industry colleagues who agree to comment on each of your posts, and you do the same in return. You can tag them in the post or in a comment to be sure they see it – just start typing their name and if you're connected, it should pop up. Each comment should be at least five words to boost the post in the algorithm.
- Tag others, including companies, by starting with the @ symbol before typing the name. Whenever I finish a speaking engagement, I now thank the company, the CEO, the meeting planner, and anyone else of note in a post on LinkedIn. You could do the same when you close a deal.

The Intellectual Philanthropist

If you want to know how to make your contact list multiply exponentially, allow me to tell you about my kind, brilliant friend Christy Lamagna.

Christy calls herself an 'Intellectual Philanthropist.' For the past several years, Christy has worked to expand her circle in a very interesting way. It started years ago with an idea: Christy decided to reach out to her five most interesting friends from different industries and different walks of life.

She asked each of those five friends, "Can you please introduce me to five people that you think are really interesting that I should meet for no other reason than to have an interesting conversation?" It started that that simply.

Her five friends probably thought, 'Knowing Christy, this is an interesting challenge. Yes, I'm going to think of five interesting people I want her to meet.'

They could be anywhere in the world, doing any job. They could be any age, any level of success.

It didn't matter to Christy, as long as they were *interesting*.

Christy's mission was simple: connect with interesting people, and then connect them to other interesting people that could be beneficial to them. Intellectual Philanthropy was born.

Christy truly has been a gift to so many people in so many organizations, because she starts every new introduction with, "our mutual friend said I had to talk with you, because you are one of the five most interesting people that she knows. I would love to have 10 minutes of your time to just talk with you."

It takes people aback because they don't believe that that is truly her motive at first, and when they realize it *is*, an interesting thing happens: they become equally philanthropic.

She asks them, "What do you need or who do you wish you knew?" or "Who can I introduce you to?" She's turned into a matchmaker of sorts, referring people who have since formed business relationships, or even friendships that have become truly amazing.

Most of them then want to reciprocate by introducing her and helping her, as she has done for them.

Since that first request years ago, Christy's circle has ballooned, and she's met some of the most fascinating people.

As a result, Christy has built this amazing network of human beings all over the planet in all different industries, and her business has thrived as a result.

It is never too early or too late for you to start being an Intellectual Philanthropist like my friend Christy. Your network will stay with you throughout your career, so think of it as one of the best investments you can make in yourself.

Good Old-Fashioned Snail Mail

The point of any sales or marketing effort is to rise above the noise to get noticed. When everyone is doing something, you have to do it differently. When few people are doing something, it's much easier to get noticed.

It's so rare today to get personalized mail. Before the Great Recession and before green initiatives, mail was booming. Everyone did mass mailers. Today, it's expensive, not green, and a waste of time unless you're sending out something truly unique.

There are two ways to do this:

1) Lumpy Mail. Nobody discards lumpy mail without opening it first to see what's inside. This can get expensive, so this is reserved for *quality* prospect acquisition, not *quantity*. I've received all kinds of memorable things in the mail – a whoopie cushion; an entire yellow-themed box with Lemonheads candy, yellow notecards, and lemon vodka; tootsie rolls and glitter; a rubber bracelet. I remember them all because they were unique and stood out from the rest.
2) Anything hand-written. 99% of the mail I receive today is pre-printed and mass-mailed, so it goes immediately into the recycle bin. Anything hand-written gets opened.

Once you've guaranteed your mail will get opened, then it's important that what's inside is compelling. Keep reading for the Seven Easy Communication Topics if you're not sure what to include.

Seven Easy Communication Topics

Now that I've discussed specific tools, I want to give you seven topics you can leverage in your communications as a strategy to easily connect on a more human level—regardless of which tool you're using.

Our culture is so splintered that it's all-too-easy to offend someone, but we still want to strive to be more personal.

Remember the fight or flight analogy? Pick one or more of these seven topics to weave into your communications to immediately put prospects into a different state of mind (Jayson did this beautifully in his cold email to me above).

These will get you far better results than pre-pandemic, overly professional business-speak.

 *Nostalgia*

If you are in a family-owned business, nostalgia is a goldmine for marketing. You can leverage old family stories, even if the business is brand new. If your company isn't family-owned, you can still leverage this in a few ways.

We can all talk about the pre-pandemic years and share good memories.

You can talk about your business in the context of the past – how past generations used your product or service.

Best of all, though, you can humanize the people who work at your company by having them share stories of their first day on the job, their childhoods, things like that. Include those in your marketing efforts.

For example, let's say you work in marketing for a hotel that's been around for 50 years. Wouldn't it be great to find couples celebrating their 50th anniversary and invite them to appear in your marketing? Or find old black & white photos of the hotel and transpose them with current ones? Or find people who stayed at the hotel through each decade and tell their stories.

Looking back is a great way to establish a company's stability, consistency, and innovation, all while telling stories of the people who made it happen along the way – both staff and customers.

 **Friends & Family**

Much of what I've been sharing in this book is about becoming more human—more relatable. What's more relatable than friends and family? Leveraging the power of this common human truth is always a great strategy. As with many other tools and strategies, though, the pandemic made stock photos and perfect-looking scenarios antiquated at best, and tone-deaf at worst.

Leverage the power of real people. How do some of your customers use your product or service? How does it enhance their relationship with their friends or family? Does it free up their time to do more of what they love? Does it give them the financial freedom to spend more time with family? Remember the adage that you don't buy a shovel because you want a shovel; you buy a shovel because you want a hole.

How can you best capture those stories? Ask your customers. Have a contest on social media, or in your store, or in your newsletter. Or hand-pick your top customers and incentivize them to share.

Gather videos of them telling about their experiences with your company. Videos are incredibly powerful, and versatile. They're far more powerful in conveying emotion and purpose than photos or writing. They're versatile because you can share them in original video form, or transcribe them into writing, or make memes – this makes them ideal. They're also the best way to capture the unmistakably authentic opinions of your real customers.

The best, most authentic format is always on a cell phone. The high production format with expensive lighting, backgrounds, and professionals is actually making those videos less relatable these days. The good news is that you can repurpose that money to other projects, and just gather simple, easy cell phone video.

 **Cats, Dogs & Babies**

My parents recently moved to a new neighborhood in an over-55 community in a suburb of Phoenix. Oftentimes, the ground is too hot for their 'dog,' Molly. I put 'dog' in quotation marks because it's an ongoing joke with them. Molly is a designer-type dog, a Maltepoo, who is all of six pounds. My Golden Retriever, Henry, considers her more of an hors d-oeuvre than a fellow dog…but I digress.

When the ground is too hot for Molly, *they push her around in a baby carriage*. At first, I thought this was absolutely ridiculous (and really still do), but it turned out to be a brilliant way for them to connect with their new neighbors. As Marilyn and Ray stroll their 'dog' around the neighborhood, all the neighbors come up to take a peek, and start a conversation. They've made quick friends in their new neighborhood as a result.

The point of this story is that pets and babies are great ice breakers and conversation starters. They humanize us all, and break through the 'us vs. them' mentality of marketing and sales.

I encourage marketers everywhere to leverage this in their strategies. More than ever, this pandemic made us crave normalcy, humanity, and connection. Pets and babies give us that.

I would caution you to avoid stock photos of happy families and dogs, though. Remember from the previous section that we're also craving authenticity. Nothing about stock photos conveys authenticity.

Use your own staff and customers, their dogs, cats, and families (with their permission, of course). Make them the stars of your advertising. Give them a face and a name. Humanize your business from your website's About Us page to your newsletter to your social media posts. Human faces breed human connection. Real humans, not models.

Case Study

WARNING!!...political example coming...WARNING!!

Please ignore your political affiliation for a couple minutes to understand the lesson I'm sharing. Here's a great example of how a political candidate differentiated himself by including his dog in a marketing video. This appeared on TikTok, and the candidate appealed to that demographic beautifully by dressing casually and talking normally.

Watch this:

 bit.ly/youtubeshawna5

My sales assistant, Rachel, had her second baby in 2021 and was over the moon. Motherhood has been a dream of hers and it's such a huge part of who she is. She's been with me for several years, and when she had her first baby two years ago, I asked if she would be comfortable including a picture of the two of them on my website and in her email signature block. She was very happy to do so.

From that moment, everything changed. Her prospecting became far more effective. It started with the occasional email reply, commenting on her adorable photo in the signature block. As time went by, she felt more comfortable mentioning her baby in her emails, and it allowed her to talk like a normal human being.

Her prospecting emails became friendlier, more conversational, and far more effective. It was a live case study happening before our eyes.

Women, especially, of all ages ooh and ahh and immediately drop their guard. Rachel is someone they immediately relate to and like, as opposed to someone they want to ignore because she's trying to sell them something (gasp).

That was a sales example, but the same applies for your marketing. You just may not notice it on a person-to-person level because you're marketing to the masses, but it's happening. People are reacting differently because you're humanizing your own people by allowing them to show that they have lives outside of work, just like your customers do.

In the post-pandemic era, there's less desire from your customers to separate their work and home lives, so why not respond in kind? Empower your own staff to share their humanity – to blur the lines between their home and work selves. It feels weird and risky, but I promise you, your customers are already way ahead of you so it's time to make this move.

 Moving Forward

Many of us were stuck in limbo for an entire year during the pandemic. As a professional speaker at live conferences, I was grounded – unable to do my job unless it was virtual. I was longing—seriously longing—to get on an airplane and get as far away from Minnesota as I could (especially in winter).

In addition to traveling, many of us were longing for the days when we could dine indoors, see a basketball game in person, or go to a concert. I had *front row tickets* to see my (imaginary) boyfriend, Adam Levine, and his band Maroon 5. The concert was postponed, and eventually canceled. I'm still mourning that one. But again, I digress...

My point is that looking forward is a great strategy over the next couple years as we continue to emerge from the dark time of the pandemic. We were all static for a period of time, and now we can finally move forward. Capture that feeling in your marketing for a sure win.

As with the other strategies herein, real stories from real people are best. How about a contest to capture those stories from customers or staff? What were/are they most looking forward to doing in the next year thanks to your product/service/company?

Really, it doesn't even have to be related to your product/service/company to catch the attention of your target market. It's all about rising above the noise for recognition, brand awareness, and the association with something positive. Share those stories with your audience. Drip them out on social media and your other channels of communication.

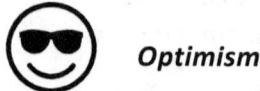 ***Optimism***

Hope and optimism are a great strategy – whether in dark times or good times. How does your company spark hope? Maybe you produce the most boring widget on the planet. You can still inspire optimism to capture the attention of your target market.

Can you partner with a great charity? Can you share stories of staff people who've overcome great odds in their personal lives? Or pick out a local hero and shine a spotlight on them once a week or month to establish a stronger local presence.

Regardless of how you share optimism, it's always a win.

 ***Humor***

Humor is my favorite communication tool. Throughout my life, it's been my way of coping in difficult times. It's how I help others cope. It's also how I embarrass my kids on a regular basis for yuks.

Next time you visit any of your own social media channels, take note of what captures your attention most. I bet humor is way up there.

Regardless of what you're marketing, there are ways to incorporate humor. Well, maybe not a funeral home, but everything else (frankly, I like the challenge of helping someone with some funeral home humor, too).

If you're at a loss as to how to find the humor in what you're marketing, ask your customers. Ask your staff. Ask your mastermind group. It's there to be found.

Heck, if you can't find *anything* funny about what you market, that in itself is funny. "Our widget is so boring, we have to schedule office laugh breaks throughout the day just to cope." Thanks folks, I'll be here all week. But don't try the veal. They're baby cows, yo!

 *Sports*

Is there anything more universal than friendly competition? Your local sports team is always great fodder for marketing fun. Of course, you have to be careful of licensing and such, but not with the local high school or middle school teams! How impactful would it be if you highlighted a monthly kiddie league sports team (with parental permission, of course), or their coach, in your marketing?

You could ask your staff or customers to share stories of their favorite sports experiences or memories. That ticks off several strategies: Sports, Family/Friends, Nostalgia, maybe more!

In Summary...

If you're in a marketing slump, challenge yourself by picking two of the above strategies and figuring out how to incorporate them into your next campaign. The entire point is to make your communications more relatable and noticeable to rise above all the marketing noise from your competition, and every other company in your customers' eyes and ears and brains. They're overloaded these days, so whatever you can do to stand out is the key to building awareness and likeability.

Eight Strategies to be More Memorable in Marketing

This section is for my homies in marketing. But sales professionals, don't tune out, because these strategies absolutely will help you in your prospecting as well.

Here are eight ways that you can be more memorable in your communications. Some of these might seem obvious if you've been in marketing awhile, but this will serve as a refresher and hopefully give you some ideas for when you're in a rut (hey, it happens).

1. Humor

I'll start us off with a doozy. This first strategy is a video you absolutely need to see. Go on and watch it right now. I'll wait.

 bit.ly/youtubeshawna1

You watched it, right? Because if you just skipped over it, your day will be less great. It's that powerful.

This video that doesn't even use a single word of dialogue. Just amazingly done. How could you not laugh along with her? She is just so joyful. It just makes me smile.

I watch this video sometimes when I need cheering up, because humor—especially throughout the pandemic—was a saving grace for so many of us.

I spoke about humor previously in this book, but it bears repeating. Humor makes whatever we're marketing more memorable.

This brilliant commercial told an entire story with no dialog. Humor is such a unifying human emotion, yet not many regular companies want to use humor or take that risk in their marketing. Why not?

What is human about your company or what you're marketing? There's got to be something that you can make fun of, or find humor in, or even be a little self-deprecating…which brings me to my next marketing strategy.

2. Transparency

Being completely transparent makes what you market more memorable. Take, for example, a tourism destination that has some innate marketing challenges. Their weather sucks.

Most of the year. Rather than doing what most destinations do and painting a false picture, check out this brilliant video:

 bit.ly/youtubeshawna3

Can you even imagine putting that out there? How did they get that word at the end past the CEO who probably was like, "We can't say that in our ad." Man, that was a huge risk.

Even though this video turned out to be a spoof, it ironically paid off tremendously for the destination as far as visibility and likeability. Not many people outside of Canada had ever even heard of that part of North America, but now I bet it's on a lot of travel bucket lists, like it is on mine.

In fact, check out the entire Newfoundland & Labrador Tourism YouTube channel for hundreds of great examples of humanized content, great storytelling, and overall blue-ribbon marketing. You can find it here:

bit.ly/ShawnaNLTourism

I'm not suggesting you have to go as far as that commercial did, but what do you see as a marketing challenge that you can turn into a marketing asset through transparency?

For example, take Minnesota. When the Super Bowl was here in 2018, our state could have said, "Oh, the weather will be fine!" but you know that's not true. The weather in February is not fine. The weather in Minnesota is not fine most months of the year.

So instead, Minneapolis embraced that and decided to run with it, rather than avoid it or paint a false picture. There was an entire campaign called The Bold North.

The city purposely had activities outside. They turned our whole pedestrian mall in downtown

Minneapolis into this showcase with all kinds of cool attractions. They're like, "Yeah. It's going to be cold. We embrace it here. We encourage you to do the same thing." Rather than telling half-truths about what the reality was, they embraced it. The people of Minnesota went nuts for it. We are the butt of so many cold-weather jokes – it was nice for a change to feel bold, empowered, and proud of our weather.

So think about what you can do. What do you normally try to sweep under the rug? What can you reframe and just say, "Yeah, this is how it is, and we love it this way." For bonus points, use humor and transparency like the Newfoundland commercial did to be far more memorable.

Do you think I'd be so excited to go to Newfoundland (or ever really would have been able to identify it on a map) without that commercial rising above the noise to capture my attention?

3. Surprise

The next strategy that is going to help you to be more memorable is the element of surprise. I want to share a story where the hero is not who you think it's going to be. The protagonist of this story got huge visibility and business from this.

KFAN is a sports talk radio station out of Minneapolis. One of their morning guys is Chris Hawkey. He's a pretty popular figure on the sports scene here in Minnesota.

Well, every year, the morning team competes against each other in fantasy football. The loser of the season has to do something terrible. One particular year, they decided that the loser had to ride home from a convention in Las Vegas—on a Greyhound bus—all the way back to Minneapolis, which is a couple days of pure hell, as I see it.

Sadly, Chris Hawkey lost the bet, and he had to ride home on this Greyhound bus. He was ticked off about this. He was bitter about it, and he posted it all over social media. He already had thousands of followers on Twitter, but this story went viral.

Tweet #1 from Chris Hawkey:

Chris Hawkey @Chris_Hawkey · Mar 31

Dear @GreyhoundBus really glad that I paid extra for priority seating just to have a lady at the counter tell me "that don't matter." (Direct quote). I'm in the next to last row. Also, the electricity doesn't work on this bus either. Terrible #CharchChallenge #HawkonAGreyhound

So far no response from Greyhound. Then...

Tweet #2 from Chris Hawkey:

He's starting these hashtags. Thousands of people are starting to follow along. The responses that he's getting are more and more like, "Oh my gosh. That's so terrible what you're going through."

Tweet #3:

Still not a peep from Greyhound, but plenty of chatter on Twitter. Can you hear that sound? It's the distant sound of Greyhound's reputation getting further crushed.

Tweet #4:

Chris Hawkey @Chris_Hawkey · Mar 31
Sunrise...sunrise.... 7a in Denver. First bus change is coming. #CharchChallenge #HawkonAGreyhound

Man, Chris looks absolutely miserable. But then something incredible happens...

 **Chris Hawkey**
@Chris_Hawkey

Oh. My. Lord. You won't believe this. Please watch. #charchchallenge #hawkonaJEFFERSON

Stop reading and watch this video for the great outcome of this crazy bus trip:

 bit.ly/youtubeshawna4

Isn't that just the best surprise? Chris and his fans went berserk!

Jefferson Lines was not a well-known bus line. Greyhound is to buses as Kleenex is to tissues. Not many people had probably ever even heard of Jefferson Lines. Greyhound wasn't paying attention to their own social media, or they were unsure what to do, so they did the worst thing: they stayed silent. They could have had fun with this. They could have been transparent and turned this around.

But Jefferson Lines was paying attention. So the element of surprise was that Jefferson Lines, on the spur of the moment—without a plan and a long, drawn-out committee decision, captured the moment. They had this bus ready for Chris Hawkey. JL for the win!

Chris made the above video that has been viewed over 100,000 times. He talked about JL so much, it was crazy. He's probably still talking about them. He changed his hashtag for that tweet to #HawkonaJEFFERSON.

Look at all the visibility for JL! This turned into such a wonderful PR move, beautifully leveraging the element of surprise. It wasn't done by Chris Hawkey. It wasn't done by Greyhound. It was done by Jefferson Lines. Now, whenever I see a Jefferson Lines bus on the road, I think back to this and what they did. It always makes me smile.

This is the kind of stuff that goes viral. And how much did this cost JL? A bus and a driver and a pizza. Not much compared to the goodwill and publicity they generated.

What can you do that creates this element of surprise? What can you do that also creates goodwill?

I don't know if you're a fan of Reddit, or if you followed the whole Gamestop drama, but I lurked on Reddit's Gamestop 'megathread' at the time. 18- to 24-year old males are the main demographic of that thread. Many of them became millionaires during the Gamestop stock squeeze.

A lot of them started doing random acts of goodwill and posting it on there, like sending chicken tenders to the staff of their local children's hospital with a thank you. The staff had to have been wonderfully surprised.

You don't have to work for a chicken tenders restaurant to send chicken to the children's hospital. And you don't have to own a bus company to be the hero of a story like Chris Hawkey's. Anybody could have sent that bus and gotten the same viral social media love. What can you do to create that element of surprise and place your company at the center of it?

4. Your Own People

Your own employees and customers can make what you market memorable. I've referred to this several times already (can you tell I'm a big fan of this strategy?) but let me share a great story with you.

 Case Study

I'd like to tell you about my friend Paul. Paul is in the type of work that gets ignored regularly. He shines shoes at the airport. There are a lot of shoeshine guys at any large airport. Nobody pays much attention to them unless they have an immediate need. Unless you need your shoes shined, you're ignoring my friend, Paul.

Well, I happened to be flying on Veteran's Day. Paul, who, by the way, happened to be 89 years old at the time, shined shoes at the Minneapolis airport because he liked to stay busy, and the extra income didn't hurt. He did that part time, because he was also a dance instructor. Do you love this guy already? Most people would never know this, because they ignore Paul most of the time.

How can a mostly-ignored shoeshine guy become a customer magnet literally overnight?

As I said, it was Veteran's Day, and Paul happened to be a World War II veteran. Yes, World War II. Paul decided, after much urging from a loyal customer, to put up a sign sharing that he's a World War II veteran. He hung, haphazardly, some red, white and blue garland on the wall. He wore his flag shirt and his cool hat.

Most people in an airport beeline to their gate unless they stop for a bite somewhere. They're

not paying much attention to their surroundings, just moving forward in a rush.

That day, Paul broke through the static, mundane routine of nearly everyone walking by. They took notice. They said, "Thanks for your service." Several people handed Paul cash, and then walked away without even wanting a shoeshine, leaving Paul in shock. Paul made more money that day than in a typical month. He also became memorable.

I checked in with Paul a month later, and he told me that people were still seeking him out. People flying out of different concourses went out of their way to give Paul their business. Lots of regular business travelers now greeted Paul as they walked by.

Paul was just one guy, no marketing team, no budget, no strategy. He just used what he had to work with – in this case himself. He took a risk, because at first he was uncomfortable drawing too much attention to himself. But looking at the outcome, I'd say the risk was well worth it.

Leveraging your own employees as part of your strategy is one of the best things you can do today to humanize them and the company. It's also one of the cheapest campaigns you could create. Plus it makes employees feel valued and seen.

How can you leverage your own people? Let me give you a few more ideas.

A Car Dealership

Car dealerships have a serious trust issue to overcome with every new customer, and they need to overcome it quickly. Most customers stepping onto a car lot have their defenses up before you even say hello.

Today, you can bet that a large percentage of your customers have visited your website before stopping by. Humanize your sales team by having them pick out their favorite car on the lot and shooting a selfie video. They could share why it's their favorite. Or ask your newest customers to share where they would take their brand new car on their ultimate road trip. Keep circulating these on your home page to immediately ease distrust and differentiate your dealership.

A Chamber of Commerce

Challenge each member to film a selfie video of their favorite business in town (aside from their own, of course). "Hey, my name is Shawna Suckow and I'm in my favorite local coffee shop owned by Rita. There's Rita. Hi, Rita! When I'm not running my own business, XYZ Company, I love to have a caramel macchiato at Rita's." Pop that video on your chamber website, and send a copy to Rita, of course.

Or spotlight different members sharing selfie videos of how they started their business, and why they chose your city.

How about offering a small prize for locals to create selfie videos of their family visiting a local business and sharing why they love it? To drive membership in the Chamber itself, ask members to do videos about the benefits they have gotten from their membership.

A Farm

Picture a corn farm in the middle of Iowa. It sells a commodity—the same product as their neighboring farms for miles and miles. How could they possibly differentiate themselves at a local farmer's market? How about posters of the people who do the work at the farm, in action?

As a teenager, my husband spent his summers de-tassling corn at a local farm for spending money (I had no idea what this was, either—I'm a city gal). How about a poster of the local teenagers who helped around the farm, a poster of the farmer harvesting the corn, and a poster of the farmer's family enjoying the corn? Or have posters of customers sharing their favorite corn recipe.

A Bank

Banks face a tough challenge for a few reasons: they are the perceived as the epitome of impersonal and institutional; they appear to be a commodity to customers; and once a customer starts a banking relationship, it's difficult to get them to switch banks, no matter how much they dislike their current bank, because of the perceived hassle.

Banks can overcome these perceptions by humanizing their institutions. Videos of customers describing how the bank supported a local cause, or helped them through a financial situation, or simply discussing why they switched banks – all these help to humanize.

A Resort

Ask customers to share their best memory on video, 60 seconds or less, about their favorite vacation at your resort.

Spotlight a different staff person each week in a video asking them why they love working there.

Regardless of what you are marketing, unleash your own team, or enlist your favorite customers. Give them an incentive to participate if you feel you need to. Start a contest on social media.

There are ways to do this that are free or dirt cheap. Really. They just take a little time and creativity. Using your own people is far more memorable than hired crew and hired models, and cellphone video is far more humanizing, which is exactly what we're going for in the post-pandemic era.

5. Throw Away the Box

There's thinking inside-the-box, then outside-the-box, and then there's my favorite: throwing away the box altogether and doing something totally different!

Inside-the-box thinking is what most of your competition does. They fit the mold of the current marketplace and don't stray too far from expectations. A smaller percentage think outside the box, trying things are somewhat different and a little risky or weird. Kudos to them. Their target audience often will take notice and subconsciously register that it's different. This is a good first step.

The next step is to be a pioneer – to do something nobody in your market or your industry has ever done. This has more risk, and way more reward when you pull it off. This is the type of stuff that goes viral.

There is so much noise out there, guys. Your prospective audience is bombarded every waking minute from every type of industry that wants a piece of their wallet. Those who are truly different rise above all that noise. Safe marketing isn't memorable, or really even noticeable anymore. Take a risk.

Take a look at this.

 Case Study

I love this story so much. The Butler County Convention & Visitors Bureau (CVB) is tasked with promoting their destination in Ohio to draw in more visitors. They're in the shadow of a big city. It's hard for them to compete because they don't have the same budget, nor the same attractions that you'd find in a much larger city. How could they possibly compete?

How could they draw visitors to their county from the big city and beyond?

Well, a few years ago, a smart staff member realized that Butler County has more donut bakeries per capita than any other county in the region, and maybe the country. So they decided to create something that had never been done before: a Donut Trail. You may have heard of the Bourbon Trail in Kentucky – that was outside-the-box thinking years ago.

Butler County, rather than try to promote the same things every single one of their competitors do (We have great restaurants! We have great hotels! We have great parks!), they not only thought outside-the-box, they threw away the box.

They created a simple donut passport that visitors could pick up at the Visitors Center in town. Visitors were encouraged to visit the 13 family-owned bakeries in town and get a stamp in their passport from each one. They could return their completed passport at the Visitors Center for a commemorative t-shirt.

At the beginning, the CVB thought they maybe would get a few people over the course of the summer to do the donut trail. So they bought a few hundred t-shirts.

Well, this concept went gangbusters with tourists, and word began to spread. They ran out of t-shirts, and the little Visitors Center was overrun. It was a huge success from the word 'go'!

Watch a video about it here:

bit.ly/youtubeshawna6

This concept has continued to explode. The Butler County Donut Trail was even featured in Food and Wine Magazine. People now come

from all over the country to visit the donut trail. It has been copycatted by several other destinations around the country with different themes. Some even blatantly copy the donut trail.

The shirts were a brilliant idea, because everybody then goes back and wears their shirt, wherever they're from. It's a conversation starter and an ongoing promoter.

Source: https://www.gettothebc.com/donut-trail

This has driven unprecedented (there's another one of those pandemic drinking words) tourism to the county, beyond their wildest dreams. Yes, of course, the 13 donut stores are loving this, but so are all the other businesses in Butler

County, and the hotels, restaurants, retailers, and other attractions.

My friends, I continue to reinforce that this does not have to be expensive. It's just taking the risk to try something new. That's the currency we're talking about that most people are afraid to spend: risk.

If Butler County had tried to compete with the bigger city, they knew that they would continue to lose. As a result of the risk they took, their visitor numbers have skyrocketed. Their marketing budget has grown, their staff has grown, and they continue to increase their t-shirt order every year. So throw away that box!

---

6. Cats, Dogs and Babies

I talked a little bit about this when I showed you the seven things that you can do in your marketing that are pretty universal right now, but certainly cats, dogs, and babies are great humanizers. Even if you're not a cat or dog person...

My dog, Henry, has become a big part of my business. I mentioned earlier that he's my Director of Barketing, and he even has his own spot on my website.

Every now and then, I include him in video emails and regular emails to prospects and clients. I include him in social media posts for my business, and he's even been in some of my YouTube and LinkedIn videos helping me teach sales and marketing lessons.

Why? Because he helps tell *the story of me*. He's part of my brand and he influences my reputation. He helps make me more memorable, because very few speakers, or salespeople in general, include their pets in their outreach. Just by that fact alone, I'm already going to be more memorable.

I hear your unspoken doubts..."What if that person doesn't like dogs?" and "What if my prospect thinks I'm unprofessional?"

Do you refuse to do business with someone because they mention in their LinkedIn profile that they like to hike, and you don't? Or you meet them for coffee, and they drive a red SUV and you hate red, so you call the whole thing off? I don't think your efforts to humanize yourself can go wrong these days (within reason, of course—if you're a nudist, keep that to yourself unless you sell sunscreen).

And the second concern – what if it makes me look unprofessional? As you've probably gathered by now from this book, that's *exactly* the point. While everyone else is busy staying professional in their outreach, you're standing out because you're taking that small risk. As for the one grump out there who really writes you off because of your dog? Well, that is far outweighed by the strides you'll make with all the others who will find you immediately more relatable, likeable, and human.

7. Your Customers

Let your customers help you tell your story. We don't always have to be the ones to tell it. My best testimonials as a speaker aren't from me saying how great I am, because guess what? That's boring, expected, and untrusted. I have my own self-interests at heart to tell you how great I am.

My best marketing is when my current and past clients tell my future customers how great I am, because they don't have skin in the game. They saw me speak, and they're going to be honest. It's going to be far more believable from that third party than it is from me.

Harness the power of your own customers to tell other customers how great your company is. Let your customers be the one to reel in those prospects by what they say about you. It's far more believable and trustworthy. Sometimes it's just a simple ask because they love you so much.

8. Weird Collaborations

Lastly, weird collaborations are wonderful and memorable. They drive traffic.

I was speaking in Hershey, Pennsylvania. I'll never forget it because of this beautiful collaboration that happened between two people in our audience that probably never would have spoken to one another without a nudge, because on the surface they were so different.

There was a man in a suit, and then there was this dude in short sleeves with tats and a scruffy beard. Yes, he was a dude! He was maybe 30, and the man was maybe 60. These two could not have been more different at first glance. Definitely not the two you would expect to strike up a conversation at a networking event.

At this particular event, I split the audience into small groups to talk about how they might be able to collaborate. These two ended up with a real-world collaboration that they ended up creating.

The 30-something guy owned a brewery. The 60-something guy in the suit owned a donut bakery (I realize donuts have become an ongoing theme of this book. I do not apologize).

These two decided to collaborate on an idea that would bring in customers on the brewery's slowest night, which was a Tuesday. They decided that they would collaborate by doing a beer and donut tasting flight – how interesting is that?

The donut guy would bring donuts to the brewery in advance so that they could use his donuts in flavoring their beer. For example, blueberry donuts would flavor a blueberry beer, and the pairing would become part of the tasting on an otherwise slow Tuesday night.

This drove ridiculous amounts of traffic to both businesses, because once they were at the brewery, they got a discount to go to the bakery at a future time. What a beautiful, weird collaboration, right?

If you manage a staff, challenge them by randomly picking an organization. Tell them you want them to come up with ways to collaborate with that organization. You might find some sparks of brilliance. At the very least, you've given your staff a chance to be creative.

SECTION FOUR
Predictions for the Future

 Get to know your 1920s phrases!

'Zozzled' Excessively intoxicated.

"Gee, Fred, I'm zozzled after that beer and sinker flight, and now I need to go iron my shoelaces!"

My Crystal Ball Says...

Traditionally, our past has informed our future. History repeats itself, and society hopefully learns valuable lessons. I've covered a lot of the similarities between the 1920s and the 2020s, but of course we have unique challenges with this century. We also have some amazing opportunities if we're willing to take that leap of faith.

I want to close this book with some predictions I foresee for this upcoming decade.

Working from Home will Continue to Empower Women, Families, and the Disabled

Covid was to blame for so much heartache and loss, but it left a few bright spots in the wake of its terrible legacy. The pandemic was the catalyst for most of the office world working from home—many for the first time.

Company leadership recognized that people *could* be as productive, if not more so, working from home. That, combined with the cost savings of needing less office space, means that this trend is here to stay. Companies that recognize this will have advantages in hiring and retention. They can hire workers from anywhere in the world, really.

"If given the choice between a $30,000 raise or permanently working from home, employees at some of the biggest companies said they would choose the latter. The Business Journals, citing a survey by professional network Blind, reports 64% of respondents would forgo the extra cash for the remote work benefits. About 67% of Google respondents preferred permanent work-from-home, as well as 64% of Amazon, 62% of Microsoft (LinkedIn's parent company), 69% of Apple, 76% of Salesforce and 47% of JPMorgan Chase employees."

www.linkedin.com/news/story/30k-raise-or-work-from-home-5059540/

Coming into the office will become more purposeful, as offices become places to meet, not just to toil away, alone in your cubicle.

> "As one business executive told me the other day, post-pandemic, if you make people come to the office, you'd better make it worth their while by emphasizing meetings, mentoring, strengthening the organizational culture and adding value through informal conversations."
> – William Fulton, https://kinder.rice.edu

The ability to work from home also will give a much-needed boost to the disabled community, opening mainstream work opportunities to those who can't commute to an office.

Additionally, this opens doors for parents of small children. We'll start to see more women remain in the workforce who no longer must choose between being a mom or an employee. More women in the workforce means more women having the opportunity to advance into leadership positions than ever before. It's high time for that, don't you think?

Lastly, working from home means your home can be anywhere. My husband works in a large corporation and never had worked from home. He's that guy who goes to the office even when he's not feeling well. Finally, thanks to his office closing for the pandemic, he realized that he can, indeed, work remotely. As a result, he was able to spend a month in Indiana experiencing the 2021 NCAA basketball tournament, while still working. As long as he gets his work done, his hours don't have to be traditional, either. His company now has an incredibly loyal employee base who proved they could have a life and be productive at the same time.

What this means for you is that your customers may work for a company in Kansas City, but decide to live in Europe, now. They might not work normal hours, because their boss doesn't require it anymore, as long as the work gets done. They'll be harder to reach, and harder to pin down for sales calls or meetings.

Shopping for Values vs. Value

We've all become painfully aware of all the small, local businesses that had to close their doors during the pandemic. Many restaurants and retailers survived solely because communities went out of their way to support them during the dark days of 2020. Others simply had no choice but to close down.

In the aftermath of the pandemic, people will see a clearer connection between where they spend their dollars and the type of retailers they want in their communities. If they want diverse, locally owned shops and restaurants, they know they have to vote with their wallets. I predict that, while Amazon continues to soar based on convenience and value, consumers will be more cognizant of small businesses who are true contributors to the local economy.

Consumers will continue to shop for value at Amazon and big box retailers but have a softer spot for the mom & pop shops than before.

We'll also see a continuation of *values*-based spending (or boycotting) when it comes to companies that take a strong stance on issues of politics (like My Pillow) religion, LGBTQ, or other divisive topics.

What does this mean for you? If you're with a locally owned or family-owned business, tell your story to build your following. If you decide to take a stand, be aware of the risks vs. rewards, as always. Be prepared, also, to constantly defend your choices on social media.

Virtual takes hold, for real this time

I was able to experience so many cool things from my living room during the pandemic: I finally saw Hamilton; I saw my (secret) boyfriend, Adam Levine and his band, Maroon 5, perform on my cellphone which I cast to my smart TV (I said that just to sound cool and techy); I did virtual yoga; learned how to make holiday pot pourri; saw two members of Whose Line is it Anyway perform a virtual comedy act; and thoroughly enjoyed a drag queen calling BINGO while performing Christmas carols from her apartment in New York.

Why, I ask you, should our ability to experience these things going forward be limited to in-person only? I predict that virtual components to live experiences will become more commonplace. Why should a Broadway show limit its production to a couple thousand people who attend in person, when they could share the experience with a million viewers across the world?

With the tough financial year from the pandemic, entertainment providers will do well to continue offering a hybrid experience: some live, some virtual.

The opportunity to see something remotely will in no way diminish the demand to see it in person. You can look at pictures of the Eiffel Tower – does that make you want to visit Paris any less? Smart live event producers will capitalize on wider audiences and greater earnings by continuing to offer a virtual component.

This will also stimulate an artistic renaissance as performers are able to reach everyday people in all corners of the world.

Fancy Dressing and Hugs

Even though I said earlier in the book that casual attire will become more common, there will be a revival of dressy attire for a short period. People have missed their nicer clothing. The problem is with the all-too-common pandemic weight gain (so I predict an uptick in sales of new dressy attire in larger sizes for a bit, haha).

Hugging and handshakes will continue to feel taboo long after we reach herd immunity, but we will grab hold anyway, despite that. We'll hold onto friends and family just a little longer and squeeze a little tighter than before. We'll also shake hands with acquaintances maybe just a little too long, but it won't be weird because they want to do it, too.

A Reset of Priorities

I know so many of us emerged from the pandemic with new priorities in life. The time spent apart from friends and family made us appreciate them all the more. I was so grateful to have my immediate family – my husband, two kids, and one of our bonus sons – home during lockdown so I didn't have to worry about them.

I used to be a road warrior. As a speaker, I loved being on the road. I bragged about the 'hat trick' whenever I had gigs in all four U.S. time zones in a month, or better yet, a week.

My time spent off the road made me antsy for the first two months; but once I settled in, I gained a new appreciation for being a homebody. Going forward, I'm limiting myself to two out-of-town speaking engagements per month. I know I'm not alone in wanting more quality time with family, and less of the constant go-go-go from before. I only wish I had realized it sooner, while my kids were still young. Better late than never.

How are you different now? How have your priorities shifted? How will you show up in the Roaring Twenties?

Hey there! You finished it! Did you like it? I would be ever-so-grateful if you would write an Amazon review to help me out! ★★★★★

From the Author

I'm sitting here on my nephew's birthday, in tears. Jack LaFollette, a 24-year old healthy, vibrant, active member of the Air Force, passed away in 2019 unexpectedly from an undiagnosed heart virus. I miss him all the time.

I started writing this book in April of 2020 and just couldn't make progress. I had the Pandemic Blahs. Every week, my poor assistant Rachel would text me to ask, "How's the book coming along?" Every week I would ignore her or send her a funny meme instead of an answer (Sorry, Rachel!).

Fast forward to first quarter of 2021, and I still was not working on the book. My friend, Christy Lamagna (the Intellectual Philanthropist you met in an earlier chapter), suggested that I pick a special date to finish the book. I picked Jack's birthday. I made a promise to Jack in my mind that I would finish it for him, and I did it.

Jack would have been 26 today. Somewhere, he's saying, "[Expletive] [Expletive] Aunt Shawna, it's about damn time!" Did I mention he was in the Air Force?

So Jack, I did this for you when I couldn't do it for myself. I will now go have a nasty shot of Jagermeister in your honor.

About the Author

Shawna Suckow, CSP (Certified Speaking Professional), CVP (Certified Virtual Presenter), CMP (Certified Meeting Professional), is a speaker with some serious knowledge of the customer mindset. She was a corporate buyer for 20 years.

Along the way, Shawna became intrigued with how customers of all kinds were evolving and responding to (or ignoring!) different sales & marketing efforts. She became obsessed with researching and sharing this insider information to sales and marketing audiences to pull back the curtain, so to speak. She realized that when these professionals had the up-to-the-minute understanding of their customers' mindsets, they could break through the noise more effectively.

Shawna has shared her research on 5 continents in 17 countries, using real case studies and data interpreted with candor and humor. Her mission is to help audiences understand the ever-evolving customer landscape – now more than ever.

What she's proud of:

- in 2019 she received the highest designation a speaker can earn (CSP©) – up to a 10-year process and achieved by less than 5% of speakers worldwide

- This is her fifth book! And hopefully her third best-seller! Fingers crossed…

- In 2020 she received the *Iconic Woman* award from the global Women's Economic Forum

Three memorable things about Shawna:

1. She's below average at the Minnesota sport of curling. Probably because she's never tried it.

2. She can do the MC Hammer dance pretty well.

3. Although it will make her wildly unpopular, she hates bacon.

Acknowledgements

Special thanks to Christy Lamagna for the push I needed. You've always been a great support. Thank you, Rachel, for sticking with me even when I frustrate the hell outta you. Mimi & Kim, you gals made the pandemic more bearable, and constantly reminded me that it was okay for me not to be in work mode. Your support these past years has made a huge difference in my career, and my personal life, and I love you dearly. To Will – thanks for spending more time with your ol' mom these past several months – they have been priceless to me. Clam, you make me proud every day. Thanks for the lockdown time. Karlin, what would I do without you? Thank you for always sharing your amazing wisdom, for laughing and crying with me, and for never judging. To my SFP Bonni (a wee, pocket-sized ninja), I couldn't have survived the mental rollercoaster of the pandemic without you. And lastly, but not leastly, Loopy – you're my constant cheerleader and you helped me get through 2020 in so many ways. Eep, op, ork, ah-ah. All of you, and so many more I didn't mention, make my life better.